D0130862

First-hand Science

Materials

Lynn Huggins-Cooper

Illustrated by
Shelagh McNicholas and David Burroughs

A⁺
Smart Apple Media

First published in 2003 by Franklin Watts
96 Leonard Street, London EC2A 4XD

Franklin Watts Australia
45-51 Huntley Street
Alexandria, NSW 2015

Series editor: Rachel Cooke
Art director: Jonathan Hair
Design: James Marks

Published in the United States by Smart Apple Media
1980 Lookout Drive, North Mankato, Minnesota 56003

Library of Congress Cataloging-in-Publication Data

Huggins-Cooper, Lynn.
Materials / Lynn Huggins-Cooper ; illustrated by
Shelagh McNicholas and David Burroughs.
p. cm. — (First-hand science)
Summary: Describes the various materials that a
family uses to prepare for a party, the characteristics
and states of the materials, and how they can be
recycled afterwards.
ISBN 1-58340-448-1
1. Materials—Juvenile literature. [1. Materials. 2.
Matter—Properties.] I. McNicholas, Shelagh. II.
Burroughs, Dave, 1952- III. Title.

TA403.2.H54 2004
620.1'1—dc22   2003058966

9 8 7 6 5 4 3 2 1

Contents

Alex is having a party! Discover all the different materials he uses.

Materials can be:

Hard

Soft

Smooth

Rough

Shiny

Bendy

Squashy

Party decorations

Alex and his sister Bethany are making party decorations. They have collected all sorts of materials.

Materials are what things are made of.

Alex has made a rocket. Bethany is making things from clay. Dad blows up balloons.

We can bend and stretch some materials.

Balloons stretch when you blow them up.

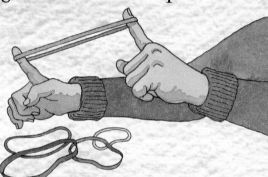

Rubber bands stretch.

You can bend and stretch clay into different shapes.

What other materials can you bend and stretch?

7

It is going to be a barbecue party. Alex and Bethany are making a picture menu. Alex cuts out rough sandpaper to make the buns.

Some materials are rough. They can be:

bumpy like corrugated cardboard

or scratchy like sandpaper.

Some materials are smooth. They can be:

soft like cloth

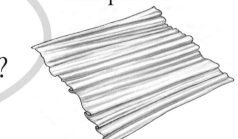

or slippery like cellophane.

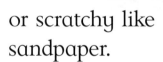

What other rough or smooth materials have Alex and Bethany used?

8

Bethany uses some soft, brown cloth to make the burgers.

Are smooth things always soft?

Some materials are soft.

Cotton

Fur

Wool

Some materials are hard.

Stone

Metal

Wood

Some materials are **solids**.

Wood is a solid.

Sand is a solid.

Chocolate is a solid, unless you heat it— then it **melts**!

Some solids melt when you heat them. They become **liquids**.

Cooking the food

Alex is making chocolate crispy bars for the party. First, Mom has to melt the solid chocolate.

I'll melt the chocolate in a bowl over hot water.

Some materials are liquid.

Water is a liquid.

Oil is a liquid.

Melted chocolate is a liquid.

Liquids are runny. They can be poured and take on the shape of the container they are poured into.

Mom pours the liquid chocolate over the bowl of crispy cereal. Alex stirs the mixture together and pours it into a pan.

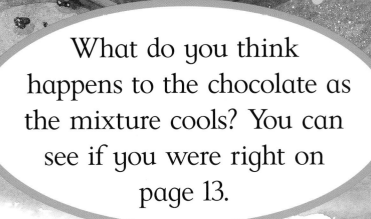

What do you think happens to the chocolate as the mixture cools? You can see if you were right on page 13.

Bethany and Dad are making a cake. They beat air into the mixture so the cake will be light and fluffy.

Air is a mixture of gases. A **gas** is another form a material can take.

Air fills up the space all around you. Breathe in and feel it filling up your lungs.

When you beat a cake mixture, you trap little bubbles of air inside it.

Gases take the shape of the container that holds them.

Alex has made popsicles with chopped fruit and juice. Now Mom puts the molds in the freezer. Alex checks his chocolate crispy bars.

The mixture is hard now.

Some liquids change to solids when you cool them.

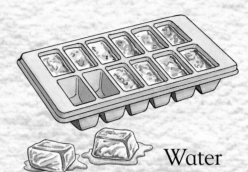

Water changes to a solid when you **freeze** it. We call frozen water **ice**.

Melted chocolate turns into a solid again when it cools.

What do you think will happen to Alex's popsicles in the freezer?

Some materials can change from a liquid to a solid—and back again!

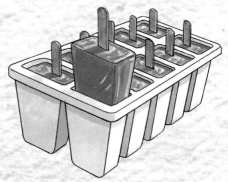

Alex's juice popsicles will quickly melt if they are taken out of the freezer. The juice contains lots of water.

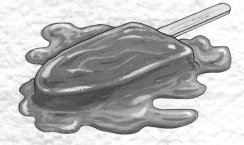

Water is a liquid. It freezes to make solid ice. The ice melts to become water—a liquid—again.

It's changed!

A few hours later, Alex checks the popsicles. They are frozen solid. He leaves them in the freezer for later.

Put them back, Alex. You don't want them to melt!

What shape will the popsicles be when Alex first takes them out of the mold?

Some materials change when they are heated and cannot be changed back again.

The cake has baked into a soft, springy solid. It can't be changed back.

When an egg is cracked, it is runny.

When it is fried, it changes from a liquid to a solid. It cannot be changed back.

The cake is baked. Alex and Bethany are making sugar icing decorations for it.

Is the sugar icing a solid, a liquid, or a gas? How else would you describe it?

The bubbles in fizzy drinks are a gas.

If you shake a bottle of soda and open the top, you make a mess! All the gas rushes out of the bottle, and it takes the liquid with it.

16

Fizzy drinks

Now it's time for a rest! Alex and Bethany have a drink of lemon soda. They watch the bubbles of gas fizz to the top of the glass.

Mom and Dad wait for their hot drinks to cool down. Dad's glasses steam up!

What do you think happens to **steam** when it touches a cold kitchen window?

Liquids can change to gases and back again.

When you **boil** water, it turns into a hot gas called steam.

Steam quickly cools in the air and changes back into water droplets. These "steam up" cold windows and glasses!

17

Party lights

It will be dark in the yard later. Alex and Bethany help Dad put candles in glass lanterns. Dad lights one to show how the light shines through the glass.

Be careful around candles, and never play with matches!

Some materials are see-through—or **transparent**—like the glass used to make windows.

Some materials are **opaque**. They do not let light through, and we cannot see through them.

Some materials are not transparent but **translucent**. We can't see through them, but they still let light through, like frosted glass.

Apart from glass, what other transparent materials can you think of? Why do you think we make windows of glass?

Some of the materials on the bonfire are natural.

Natural materials are found in nature. People use them to make other things.

Wood is made into chairs, tables, and doors.

Stone is made into houses and pavement.

Wool is made into clothes, blankets, and carpets.

Build a bonfire

Alex, Bethany, and Dad are building a bonfire.

They pile up old leaves, wood, and some cardboard boxes.

Don't put plastic on the fire. It makes nasty fumes.

Look around the room you are in now. Which materials are natural and which are made by people?

Other materials are made by people. People use natural materials to make new materials.

Many plastics are made from oil.

Paper is made from wood.

Glass is partly made from sand.

Some materials burn very easily.

Paper

Straw

Wood

 Oil

Other materials do not burn.

Stone

Glass

Metal

Party time!

The guests have arrived! The fire is lit and so is the grill. Mom lights the candles in the lanterns.

Everyone stands well back from the bonfire. Dad has buckets of sand and water nearby just in case.

Fires can spread quickly and can be very dangerous.

To keep safe, people use:

Fireguards

Fire blankets and buckets of sand

Never play near bonfires or open fires. Fire burns you!

Fire extinguishers

23

Some materials heat up quickly, as heat passes through them easily. Metal heats up quickly.

Pans are made of metal. They heat up quickly to cook things.

Some materials don't get hot so easily.

Pan handles are often made of wood. It does not heat up as quickly as metal, so we don't burn our hands!

It's really dark now and getting cold. Mom has made hot chocolate for everyone. Bethany and Alex are glad they have warm coats.

What things around the home can become hot so you have to be careful not to touch them? What materials are they made of?

Some materials are good at keeping things warm.

Materials that trap air keep you warm. Your body heats up the air, and your clothes trap it around you.

Fleecy coat

Woolen gloves

Pullover

Dad has a surprise! Whoosh! Fireworks sparkle in the sky.

Always watch fireworks at a safe distance. Never touch or play with them even after they have gone off.

Not all trash needs to be thrown away. Some materials can be **recycled**.

Glass bottles and jars can be made into new containers.

Metal cans are recycled to be made into new cans.

Newspapers and magazines are recycled and made into new paper, egg cartons, and cardboard.

Some plastics can be recycled and made into flowerpots.

Cleaning up

It was a good party. The next day, the family tidies up. They sort out the trash for recycling.

Materials that are recycled aren't trash anymore—so they won't end up in big trash dumps called landfill sites.

What can the family recycle or reuse from the party?

We can reuse things, too.

Yogurt cups to plant seeds.

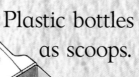

Plastic bottles as scoops.

Toilet roll tubes and boxes for making models.

27

Try this yourself

Have fun with materials!

A bathtub iceberg

Fill a balloon with water and tie the top. The water could be mixed with some food color or glitter body gel. Put it in the freezer and leave it for a few hours, until the water is frozen. When the balloon feels hard, remove it from the freezer and ask an adult to tear the balloon off the ice. Now float the "iceberg" in a bathtub of warm water. How long does it take the iceberg to melt? Your bath water will cool down as the iceberg melts, turning from solid ice back into liquid cold water.

The garbage gobbler

You can make a monster trash can to help you keep your room tidy. Decorate a plain plastic wastebasket with scraps of yarn, tagboard, fabric, plastic packaging, or egg cartons, using strong hobby glue. You can make your monster as horrible as you like, but remember to make a big open mouth to put the trash in!

Chocolate heaven

Ask an adult to help with this, as it uses heat.

Break up a big bar of chocolate, then ask an adult to melt it in a microwave or over a bowl half filled with hot water.

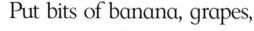

Put bits of banana, grapes, strawberries, and marshmallows on toothpicks. Dip them in the liquid chocolate and then put them on a plate. As the chocolate cools, it will turn back into a solid—and you can have a feast!

Useful words

boil: To heat a liquid to the point where it bubbles and changes into a gas.

freeze: To cool a liquid so it changes to a solid.

gas: Some materials are gases. They do not have their own shape and spread out to fit any space they are held in.

ice: Frozen water.

liquids: Some materials are liquids. They can be poured and take the shape of the container they are held in.

materials: Materials are what things are made of.

melts: To heat a solid so it changes to a liquid.

opaque: Light cannot pass through opaque materials.

recycled: To make new materials from ones that have already been used.

solids: Some materials are solids. They have their own shape.

steam: The gas water becomes when you boil it.

translucent: Translucent materials let light through but are not easy to see through.

transparent: Transparent materials are see-through.

About this book

This book encourages children to explore and discover science in their local, familiar environment—in the home, school, garden, or park. By starting from "where they are," it aims to increase children's knowledge and understanding of the world around them, encouraging them to examine objects and living things closely and from a more scientific perspective.

Familiar materials and their properties are examined, along with states of matter, reversible and non-reversible changes, and recycling. This is done in "child friendly" terms, using questions to build on children's natural curiosity and encourage them to think for themselves. The aim is to lay a strong foundation for the readers' future learning in science.

Index